SIX SHADES OF NATURE

SEASONAL HUES OF SERENE VERSES: A COLLECTION OF POETRY

DEEPTI AGRAWAL

The Almighty

For giving us the gift of

Beautiful Nature.

Contents

Contents

Preface

Nature is full of surprises and different hues. This book has poems from the six seasons of nature. Spring, Summer, Monsoon, Autumn, Winter along with some musings.

Change

Things have changed a lot

The world has come quite far

And so did I

Transitions of technology

Patterns of humanity

Outlook of one person to other

All has changed, Yet

The Wind, The Season, The Sun, The Moon, The Flowers, and

dreams are still the same

It's Time to forget the blues and embrace love.

Enjoy the poetic seasons here and you can even enjoy the "Shades of Emotions" , another one of my poetry publications.

"Emotions - Through the Lens of Ancient and Modern Literature" is again one of the masterpieces created, giving insights into the psychology and personality of a being.

Musings of Seasons

All around the flowers bloom

In all colors and hues

Chirping envelops the aura

Nests are seen everywhere

With the glowing hot sun

Summer sets in

With lovely mangoes and lychees

Soothing hats, umbrellas, and glares

With humid winds

Greens are all bare

Strewn across the earth

Fallen time waits to shoot

White is the color all over

With mufflers and heaters

Sun shines weakly

Spreading warmth all around

The season comes and goes

Filling our lives

With rainbows of memories

To cherish forever

Mesmerizing Nature

Mystic hues envelop the arena

Shadowed greens dances

Damsel winces at the squall

Yet! Some bright color gawps

Mesmerizing Nature Commands!!

My Home

The lovely greens of my garden

Soothing swirls of my hot coffee

Chirping sweet song of sparrows

The melody of the wind chime

The gentle sway of the swing

Intoxicates me completely.

My Home. My Pride.

Wish

Wish I could be a Tree

and feels the Earth beneath

spreading my branches free

giving shelter to all thee.

Birds make their nest

when tired, come to rest.

As green as I could be

standing calm, all by me.

Wind blows

spreading my flowers

all over the road.

When I bear fruits

feels myself, so cute

Atmosphere near me

fills with sweet fragrance

tiny little hands

all come for a chance

birds and bees fill me

chirping and jumping

all over me.

Oh! What a wish

I just had

Wish, my wish to come true

and make me all glad.

Enchanted!

Crawling on the

snake like curvy roads,

relishing every inch of

greens all around,

feasting on the fragrance

of the - dissipated wildflowers,

captivated by the cool

clouds touching the skin,

letting my hungry eyes

devour the beauty of the hills,

found myself enchanted

amidst the heavy woods! !!

Spring

1. Spring Time

Vacant thoughts engulf me
on a solitary spring morning
mesmerizing with its beauty.
gleeful chirping birds
making a home on trees
shepherds are busy
stalking their herd
squirrels are jumping
merrily - tree to tree
tiny skillful ants
trespassing my backyard
marigold is in full bloom
emitting fragrance all around
shining smiling sun is
enveloping the ground.

2. Mystic Spring

I see blue, green, and pink
In me, let the fragrance sink
Butterflies flutter their wings
All around me the bird sings
The birds, the bees, and the caterpillar
Makes my life a bit more fuller
Spectacular spring smiles
I see beauty for some miles
Magic of colors spread
Pearls of flowers get, thread
Dewdrops on a leaf sparkles
Happiness inside me crackles
Sparrows, cuckoos, and robins
Exuberant I, go for tailspins
Magical Elixir of life lifts
I see myself in high spirit.

3. MAGIC IN MARCH

Mesmerized by blossoms
All around
Gazing beautiful bounty
Indulging in the
Calmness smeared around
Inspired by the colors
Numbing the senses
Motivated by new energy
Aggregating magic of fragrance
Remembering meaningful
Conversations whispered in
Happy mellow hearts.

4. Butterfly

Flying high, being a butterfly
sings aloud in deep forests
let me drink the nectar to my full
seems like it was made just for me!
When I open my Rainbow wings
smiles, feeling elated
heights of that high sky
it's that, Now I want to touch it!!

5. Humming Bird

From a flower to flower
She hums her way
Sucking nectar
Spreading smiles
Fragrant buds welcome

.

.

The musical notes drift
Her fluttering wings hum
Harnessing completely
Happily rejoicing
The heaven and earth

~ ~

Summer

Enter Caption

6. Nature

Scorching burning sun
Sweltering the arena
Itching blisters
Oozing vermilion
Thick dark clouds hover above
Waiting to burst open
Screeching whimpering winds
Jettisoning everything
Soothing cool rain
Washes away the burns
Emitting aromatic aroma
Comforting within.

7. Mango Season

It's time for mangoes and more
Season of bright sun and humid air
Roads are empty and plenty of time to spare
Dusty lanes and crispy leaf
All waiting for the rain to slip
Pregnant clouds hover above.

8. Withering Summer

With prickly sweat
Trickling down the spine
Finding respite
Under the Neem tree
Quenching thirst
With sweet cool lime
And syrupy watermelon
Oozing nectar from
Green coconut
Tastes like Heaven
Juicy mangoes tease
Oh! I want some more, please!
Scorching sun
Reverberates its heat
Let the 'Matka Kulfi' melt
And beat the sizzling heat
Sun Flowers stand valiantly
Shinning in the sun
Summers are here
Now waiting for the Rain.

9. Summer

The bright strong sun smiles
Splashing the vibrant summer
Parched Earth awaits
Little footsteps gather mangoes
Carrying bucket full of loads
Hurrying footsteps runs
Towards the soothing shades.

Monsoon

10. Rains

Impregnated cloud burst open
Rupturing its water bag
Drenching the terrain
Parched scars repaired
Extraordinarily
Giving birth to fresh greens
Rainbow streaked its color
Budding new flora
Tiny feet splashed
Excitedly at the puddles
Breathing at the moment
Living to the fullest.

11. Monsoon

Oysters are waiting
for the first drop
to change it in a pearl
one day it will adorn
the finger of a girl...
That little seed is
looking up for the moisture
to help it bloom
in a beautiful tree
to borne fruits for free..
wait is over
monsoons are here
to quench our thirst
bringing respite from the heat
moistening our feet...
I can -
smell the rain
see the trees dancing
hear the clouds rocking
feel the sweat evaporating
taste the fresh Monsoon....!!!

12. Just the other day

Just the other day
looking out of my window
I saw
a baby bird learning to fly
queen bee trying to reach the sky..
I found
a pregnant cloud, hovering over
waiting to bring in a shower..
I cherished
the moments to see the bud
blooming in the beauty..
I longed
to satiate my thirst with
the dew drops on leaves..
I cried
wanting to belong
just the other day at my window......!

13. Zenith

When heaven poured down
Cleansing every nook and corner
Vaporizing the afflictions
Spreading warmth all around
Sun reaches its Zenith
Revitalizing all around

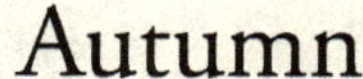

Autumn

14. Vacuum

Thick white clouds on
a solitary morning
settled on the garden-bench
leaving it misty and wet
for a long long time.
engulfing vacant calmness
was smeared on the trees.
Purple, White, Yellow flowers
laced with the cold dew
look crumpled under the sun.
early buds of the grass
strewn on the brown flower bed
were crushed by
the hurried footsteps
of no significant destination.
baby sparrows and squirrel
quarrel over a tiny piece
of grain resting on the
windowsill for long,
all drenched in the night rain.
fallen leaves of neem tree
lie scattered all over
sensing the

deadly stillness of
within and without.

15. LAVENDER BLOOMS

Longing aches deep inside

Arousing throbbing sensations

Vacuums the feelings

Enduring pain persists

Nurturing the abyss

Drumming intimate

Echo of silence

Reverberates

Bulging emotions

Live to breathe

Omitting the intense niggle

Overlapping

Meaningful

Significance!!

LAVENDER BLOOMS procures memories!!

16. Into the woods

Walking down the by lanes
Of lost times
Footsteps found the path
Into the woods
Sitting under an old tree
Thoughts unfold
Spreading their wings
Showing colors
Bringing smiles from within
Life is Beautiful …. Indeed!!

17. Mundane Influences

On a solitary day
Once green now yellowed
Descended with the flow
Words littered
Hither and thither
In the waking of a sound
Pinks and purple hues
Gallantly peered
From the parched patch
Whispering coos
Resonated around
Satiating yearning
Crunchy crisp browns
Sear the image
Of absent Bygone.

Winter

Enter Caption

18. Winter Rains

Washed up in winter rains
Petunia, Pansy and Zinnias
Smiling swaying valiantly
Enjoying contentedly
Splashed up by morning rain
Garden greens beaming
With soaring high heads
Glistening portentously
Smeared with dew drops
Daylight peeped mystically
Filling in with all its pride
Blushing as a new bride
Streaked with the chill
Warm breath radiated
Pleasing the senses
Dissolving in winter rains

19. In The Snow

Soft cotton swirled
Melting with the touch
Resting on the nose as soft as rose
Winter chill sweeps inside
Turning the garden white
Tiny footsteps tread
Dancing on the ground
'Tis time to build new snow fairies
When new dreams surmount
Soothing music surrounds.

20. Nightingale

On the top of that 'Gulmohar' tree
She rested her tired wings
At dusk when all returns
She found a cozy spot
At the first hint of dawn
She chirped merrily
Bringing life all around
Spreading happiness
Her melodious song
Fills all with tranquility
Oh! How I wish to sing like her
My pretty Nightingale
Her music stirs something
Deep inside my soul
To be close to nature
And reconcile is what I wish!!

21. Winter chills

Time for a few Goodbyes'
Long grumpy days
And sweltering sun
Parched wallowing earth
Chameleons and squirrels
Resting for a season
Stuffing with ample sustenance
Working on a silence
Fresh new green sprouts
Peaking buds blossom
Emanating intoxicating fragrance
Melodious chirpings drifts
Bringing in first chills
Dewdrops sparkles
On velvety shining grass
Heady sensations surface
Rejoice ....
Winter chills are here again.

Shades of Nature

BREEZE

Fragmented calm and soothing breeze

Gently, caressing her silken tresses

Filling her with happiness.

STORM

Growling air, filled with dust

Gushes and destroys everything on its way

Calmness follows, like a deathly hallow.

TORNADO

Angry wind full of lust

Invades the innocent and calm nature

Leaving behind – ruined serenity all over.

RAIN

Droplets of water

Satiates the greedy earth

Quenching its thirst.

About The Author

Deepti Agrawal is an Author of four books in her name and published her work in ten Anthologies other than several E-Magazines and platforms, Her books have found prestigious place in many libraries along with few awards for her work.

She, being a Healer, finds herself close to nature and gets inspired from it. Her art works, stories, poetry, etc all have a close connection with Nature. She weaves magic with the spools of imagination. Also, Her work is well-researched and enhanced with anecdotes from her life and around which are presented with experience.

Deepti Agrawal

More From The Author

1. Shades of Emotions : *A Collection of Poetry* - having all basic Nine shades of emotions separated and weaved together to experience every emotion at its best.

2. Emotions - *Through the Lens of Ancient and Modern Literature*

3. Rasgatha (Hindi) - Stories of nostalgic village tales, unknown or forgotten people, sensitive beings, inspiration, pain, decisions, innocent lives, and much more are into this telltale 'RasGatha'.

4. Hope- A potpourri of Short Stories and Poems by Payal Agarwal and Deepti Agarwal